Friday Night, Shanghai

poems by

Arthur Solway

Finishing Line Press
Georgetown, Kentucky

# Friday Night, Shanghai

Copyright © 2023 by Arthur Solway
ISBN 979-8-88838-272-1 First Edition
All rights reserved under International and Pan-American Copyright Conventions.
No part of this book may be reproduced in any manner whatsoever without written permission from the publisher, except in the case of brief quotations embodied in critical articles and reviews.

Publisher: Leah Huete de Maines

Editor: Christen Kincaid

Cover Art: Yang Fudong, *Seven Intellectuals in a Bamboo Forest, Part II—Nr. 1*, 2004, Photograph, 84 x 112 cm. Courtesy Yang Fudong and ShangART, Shanghai and Marian Goodman Gallery, New York.

Author Photo: 文海军 Wen Hai Jun

Cover Design: Elizabeth Maines McCleavy

Order online: www.finishinglinepress.com
                also available on amazon.com

Author inquiries and mail orders:
Finishing Line Press
P. O. Box 1626
Georgetown, Kentucky 40324
U. S. A.

Table of Contents

Extended Lullaby 1

The Weight of Every Possible Move 2

Yellow 3

Skin Deep 4

Andaman Morning 5

Because There's No Patron Saint for Chocolate 6

Mid-Autumn Moon 7

God and Windshield 8

A Matter of Faith 9

What Is Not 10

The Studio 11

Giacometti's Nose 12

Samuel Beckett's Tree 14

Vanitas 15

My Warhol 16

Utopia Parkway 17

Late Portrait 18

Remembering Steinberg 19

An Orchid for Robert Mapplethorpe 20

Until the Sun Comes Up 21

Where the Sky Meets the Sea 22

Postcards	23
Like Air	24
Rexroth's Dream	25
Nietzsche's Ghazal	26
Siddhartha On Fire	27
To Marie	28
Friday Night, Shanghai	29
Fu Xing Park	30
Airport Blues	31
Love Songs In Another Language	32
Shadow Nation	33
Today	34
Notes Prior To Departure	35
Tomorrow	36
Turning	37
People Like To Tell Me Things	38
Late Summer Lament	39
Anima Mundi	40
The Corners	41
Night School	42
Notes	43
Acknowledgments	44

for my daughter 邵文轩 *also known as Frances*

Change, move, dead clock, that this fresh day
May break with dazzling light to these sick eyes.
Burn, glare, old sun, so long unseen,
That time may find its sound again, and cleanse
What ever it is that a wound remembers
After the healing ends.

—Weldon Kees

Extended Lullaby

It begins in the night sky throwing coins.
Not a nocturne but a lullaby,
brushing lightly against a golden comb.

A metal wheel turning so slowly inside a box.
If you lift the lid, "No such thing
as silence," he says. "Shhh, listen

to the spores, the underbelly
of a mushroom strummed like a chord,
with a feather, a whiff and whisper

to twist a key behind your pillow.
Slower, turn it slower," the composer says,
"the tempo isn't right."

The Weight of Every Possible Move

Duchamp's apartment, circa 1970

It was how the particles of dust
in sunlight swirled and slowly fell:
how as a boy barely thirteen
he stood over the chessboard
mesmerized by its bronze pieces,
and in that late afternoon light
as if by their stillness alone
he might know the weight
of every possible move,
as if he might always be there
in this room with a woman
he would never know,
not knowing why he had come
or why he was there, if not to play
then to pay his respects
to the sunlight, to those particles
of dust floating through the air.

Yellow

        Higher,
harder,
children on the swings.
A clockwork of legs
kicking till dusk.

It's early November
when the starlings
dive through a dilapidated glow.

Streetlight is nothing like salt,
nothing like bread

as the birds
in a yellow blotch of light
peck the concrete,

and where a man
in blue, in the middle of his life,
waits on a green bench.

Skin Deep

She wanted to plant a tree
below her left shoulder.
Her skin, the earth, the color of tea—
but a history of ink is older.

Below her left shoulder
she wanted a tree with her initials,
blood-chiseled yet bolder
to make it official.

She wanted a tree with her initials,
a landmark that feels like home.
Skin deep to make it official
in indigo monochrome.

This place she'd always come
with a pair of birds, an empty swing,
the melody of a harmonium
to recall how her children sing.

A pair of birds, an empty swing.
She wanted to plant a tree
with its own history every spring.
Her skin, the earth, the color of tea.

Andaman Morning

for Michel Houellebecq

The café umbrellas bloom early
under a harsh tropical sun.
I order yellow curry
and a cold beer for breakfast.
It's almost noon.
It isn't easy to say certain things.
The clouds are like shrapnel
or with so little effort
they blow themselves apart,
charted by a certain slowness
to declare their sovereign kingdoms.
The king has died.
The tourists keep coming.
Children return to their sandcastles
as small flags along the shoreline
point us in another direction.

Because There's No Patron Saint for Chocolate

Hardheaded heart,
half an almond shell.

But you were never one to kiss
and tell,

with our red ribbons and secret
memos: dark or bittersweet?

And what a fine day to stay in bed
dreaming of fondue

while going through an entire box
of heart-shaped afflictions.

February's bullseye with its stickpins
and sometimes teardrops

the size of bonbons
smear a lover's lapel, like now.

Your complexion silky smooth, clear,
and 70% cacao! Go ahead—

eat me.
I'm forever yours,

because you're too damn cute
and I'm so Cupid stupid.

Mid-Autumn Moon

We aren't supposed to speak your name.
Not anymore. Or describe a glowing
river of clouds that drift by you like code.
Still, you manage the bright hole

through which a perfect lunacy shimmers
and without dark monologue.
We aren't supposed to use your image—
not anymore. You're beyond reach,

but you manage the brightness.
Even if you are only a hand mirror
in some nonexistent heaven,
it's easier to love you from afar.

God and Windshield

At her age, my mother always says,
life is like a train. Sometimes the ride is nice
and sometimes there are stops
we'd wish we didn't have to make.
Spoken casually, indifferently,
as if lounging beneath Buddha's tree
down along the banks of the Ohio.
What did I know?
I was a child and she looking
like she just stepped from a painting
by Alex Katz—Hermès scarf, sunglasses,
shades of Jackie O.
Into the convertible we'd go
taking the camel-humped hills
sending one's stomach to one's throat.
She'd make the accelerated curve,
punch the gas, swerve the contours
of careless laughter. The car radio blaring
against God and windshield
the jazz she so adores—Miles, Coltrane,
Parker—from a barge docked
off the Kentucky side.
"Radio Free Newport,
Home of the Jazz Ark,"
the announcer, Leo Underhill,
would holler and who she'd insist
was drunk by 10 a.m.,
while Eddie Jefferson—
you are the soul
who snaps my control—croons, *There I go,*
There I go, There I go again....

A Matter of Faith

You can count on the crows
before sunset, bickering.
This is my faith.

How they swirl the air like ink
or smudge the trees
in charcoal, out of sync

with their own shadows.
This is my faith before nightfall
as evening skies

the color of rosé
segue to black
with echoes of cruel laughter.

What Is Not

My twisted alibi, the silent who
and almighty why

or misplaced where. Or what
as in what went wrong

and when. What is not
turned sideways or backwards?

A lifeless rut, a knot,
in my most likely never

and all for naught,
not knowing if I aced the test.

Notwithstanding,
it kneels to reason

if not is the godless spot
of who I am. I forgot.

The Studio

after Philip Guston

Outside the walls of his studio
nobody could hear him,
nobody listening
where even the paint
simply dried in its sleep.

He heard himself talking
to an empty room.
The low angry stutter of the wind,
some bricks, the limbs
of a leafless tree . . .

wanting nothing to do
with him or anybody else,
but to climb through
the one and only window
where everything shook.

Giacometti's Nose

Like a saber through a box
where the head hangs
in it. A box without walls.
His first dream of death,
laid out in a glass casket
and surrounded by dwarfs.
How odd that an artist
who made a life of lean,
lanky figures would dream
a horizontal dream.
Marlene Dietrich, not Snow White,
fell in love with his sculpture
of a dog. It didn't last.
"It's me," he told Jean Genet,
who called his figures
"the watchers of the dead."
"I was the dog," he said.
In a notebook entitled
The Death of T., Giacometti
sketched the long and ugly
death of his studio assistant.
Alberto and his brother Diego
dressed the corpse.
"The head had become
an object, a little box,
measurable, insignificant,"
Alberto wrote. "A fly
approached the black hole
of his mouth, then slowly
disappeared inside."
Years earlier, as a boy
at bedside, Alberto watched
an old Dutchman bang his head
against a hotel wall.
As it shrank," he observed,

"all but his nose
seemed to shrivel into death."
Snout like an oilcan.
Nightmares he couldn't shake.
Paris, a huge spider,
or venereal disease
he'd catch at The Sphinx,
the most famous bordello
during his time.
"Prostitutes went hand in hand
with death,"
was what one biographer
remarked back then.
His mistress, Carolyn,
in Montparnasse:
"When he died," she said,
"he looked like nothing
more than one of his own."

Samuel Beckett's Tree

He wasn't finished with the tree.
He was neither tourist nor traveler.
He ate only cut fruit.
He wasn't one for all seasons.
There was great indecision about the tree.
Its limbs, its leaves? The girth, height,
and thickness of its trunk?
He wasn't finished with the tree.
And there the homeless hung out,
waiting for a sign, some word, or to rest
beneath its bareness.
He drank Calvados for the scent
of late autumn afternoons,
for burnt apples in a sunlit glass.

Vanitas

The eyes go first
as if wiped from a puddle
of old skin,
only to recall every pore

and aging dimple
at the door
of lips unlocked,
a mouth wanting more

once as smooth as river stones
tossed off a cliff,
a crooked nose, nostrils
collapsed or tunneled,

muzzled above chin and cleft,
a jawbone chiseled
then back again
to a furrowed mezzanine,

lost in time, to thought,
the mise en scéne, a penthouse
once called the skull,
to busted pulleys, rusty cogs.

My Warhol

circa 1963–1968

It's your impassive gaze, the deadpan stare.
Where the word silence hangs above the door.
There in a silver room with its only chair.

Why bother arguing about the color of the air?
No one really cares. It's perfect with this décor.
It's your impassive gaze, the deadpan stare.

What couture should a condemned man wear?
"Nothing Special" is on the tube. Life's such a bore,
There in a silver room with its only chair.

Tried for treason, but the evidence is spare.
It isn't personal—just business and nothing more.
There in a silver room with its only chair.

And what is it about the style of your hair?
Like a celebrity suicide or disaster worth waiting for …
It's your impassive gaze, the deadpan stare,

It's the look that says no one's really there
And like nothing else you've ever seen before.
It's your impassive gaze, the deadpan stare,
There in a silver room with its only chair.

Utopia Parkway

after Joseph Cornell

He spoke of neighborhood thieves and his passion for a singer
whose name we've long forgotten.
He lived on donuts.
He prowled junk shops for pictures of exotic birds
and ballerinas, old maps, a tarnished figurine.
He looked like a haggard tramp. Tramp thin.
His house was a firetrap.
He kept notes on his fixations. A naughty little man
was how Duchamp's widow described him.
The magician of the secondhand.
He was obsessed with the young girl who
lived next door. There will be many loves like this,
the gypsy fortune teller would say
until her machine went on the blink.
Her predictions were always the same.
Years ago he gave my mother a small gift,
inscribed and tied with a bow. She never opened it.
He took it back feeling unloved and bitter.
Back to the shoebox theater of his mind to rejoin
a vast collection of odd souvenirs: a rabbit's foot,
the pocket atlas, a defective compass, the tiny hourglass
from some shabby penny arcade.

Late Portrait

for Francesco Clemente

You don't need a mirror.
Any window will do.
You don't need a clock,
looking down a pair of legs
slung over the bedside.

The radio offers its sleepless voice
of a man whose face
you can only imagine. In the dark,
in dark trees, a light rain
falls to its groggy destination.

With a flick of a switch
your urgency is there
in an empty frame for light
and air. In some brash portrait
of whatever happens to pass.

Remembering Steinberg

"You are the same person," he said, "but in different perspective," when he came to the door wearing a paper bag on his face. This was 1969 on Union Square and about all I'd remember of him in those days, when the idea of some rite of passage throws me backwards and forwards in a single glance. I wonder, as the story goes, if the artist would have known how my father sold his drawings on the road. Long nights behind the wheel, smoking through Indiana and Pittsburgh, Toledo to Detroit, along the highway with its static of lonesome chatter for those hard-to-close customers as headlights traced or dashed his parallel hope, like looking down the wrong end of a telescope.

An Orchid for Robert Mapplethorpe

It comes from the Greek *órkhis*
meaning testicle.

Unlike the flowers
he didn't care much for sunlight.

He loved pictures of flowers
more than the flowers themselves.

And male genitalia,
which was his other ikebana

also known as *the way of flowers.*
A perfect specimen, the male physique.

His hothouse Hercules,
born in Floral Park

—and no, it wasn't the blood
of Nessus that killed him.

Until the Sun Comes Up

Night is a cube
configured by imperfect silence,

defined by its dimensions
for the disenchanted.

Night is a hose
with which all shadows are beaten.

Night my old heartthrob
I can't take my eyes off you.

Night is a lonely egg.
My offspring out of orbit.

We have nowhere else to go.

Night, be still.

Where the Sky Meets the Sea

How many times have you imagined a room
with whitewashed walls, a floor
of smooth stone cool to bare feet.
A room that is sparse. Only a table and chair.
There is a solitary window looking out
to where the sky meets the sea,
cloudless and blue. There is nothing else.
And how many times has an emptiness
such as this filled you with a sense of calm
too good to be true, as the setting sun
cuts water like an old knife, its amber light
casting its spell and you unafraid to say
the word: *sparkle*.

Postcards

You are thinking about imaginary postcards
from imaginary places,

small islands
where you first notice the postage stamps,

the postmarks
and dates of cancelation.

Never more than a few lines:

In one hand you rattle a tambourine,
and in the other an abacus.

These are your instruments.
These are your bones.

Then one day you return to that distant cliché
about your face on the moon.

Like Air

I spoke to the sea.
Each day
taken by hand
down to where water
is the darkest
tongue and every
word so cruel I
could cut you
as waves cut water.

We argue the quality
of time.
Like the color
of sea glass.
Like the sea itself
a blade of sadness,
never enough air.

Like all other
love lost
at sea. For each
and every rung
of air,
a ladder we climb
all hours of the night.

Rexroth's Dream

Lost in thought, he sat soaking
in the therapeutic pools.
What is it about enduring myth?
This sad and ancient legend,
now a cliché, of the Chinese poet
presumably drunk
who drowned trying to scoop
the moon from a lake.
Air tainted by a sulfurous stench
on this moonless night centuries later.
Who can I trust? he asked,
skimming the surface
in search of a face, his hands
reaching into black water
as a slight wind swept away his eyes.
Then he put his ear to the water
straining for a voice,
any voice, as his small boat
swayed as in a sleepwalker's dream.
Only the splash of a leaping fish.
Then the water went still.

Nietzsche's Ghazal

It comes to you again, the question of being human.
You've pondered the expression to be human,

all too human, but what does it mean?
Lamenting the so-called human

condition, we move through disquieting days,
scrolling images of the inhumane—

how a history of humankind isn't easily mended.
At the end of what we've called humanity

what can you tell us? Tell us it will be fine,
it'll be OK. Tell us we're only human.

Siddhartha On Fire

Think of those monks who remember that first fire,
witnesses to blistering heat, the searing stench of kerosene
as crowds gathered and novices and nuns looked on
in disbelief. Even the police. Siddhartha on fire.
And those beads around his wrists signified a sentence
of faith, a sentence in which refuge was a blazing mandala
with sprockets tooled for this one miserable wheel,
because there are no ordinary stories about suffering.

To Marie

If there's anybody I should thank it's Marie Skłodowska-Curie.
She saved my life.

So the next time I find myself in Paris
I'll head straight to the Panthéon

and bring her flowers. Or I won't.
Unless I can find a bouquet of mutant Fukushima daisies.

And while I'm there I might visit
with Voltaire or Braille, Zola and Rousseau.

But mostly with Marie.
With radium isotopes in her pocket

she liked the way they glowed
in the darkness of her desk.

My body too was once a dirty bomb.
I managed the darkness and did not detonate.

Friday Night, Shanghai

On a Friday night in Shanghai
you might find John Berryman drinking
down on Maoming Road,
where the loneliest light in the French Concession
cascades across an empty dance floor.

Even the mirror ball is confused, and clumsy
—and Berryman knew all about balls.
Never mind that the eternal nowhere is spinning
radiant circles thrown recklessly against four walls.

Never mind that the drama of beauty
can't easily be defined
as the old songs grow older, going round and round,
in the hearts of every girl and boy
on a Friday night in Shanghai.

Fu Xing Park

You have your impossible balloons.
This you know.
They, too, have a clever and final scheme.
The bumper cars are identical bullies.
There is no other way.
This you know
as the little train leaves the station
to circle its rickety kingdom
and whatever sense of wonder we have left.
But today in the hydraulic calm
of an off-key calliope and carousel ponies
you feel less electrified
knowing someday the ride will end.
There is no relief
for how you let love trip.
This is your compulsion to ruin the nest.
This is for the thief
asleep beneath the trees.
This is for the kites that got caught.

Airport Blues

My passport, a scrutinized novella
with its collection of faded anecdotes,
rubber stamps, and expired visas.

I come and go, come and go
longing for slower summer days
to be cleansed by clear light,

lying naked under cypress
or strolling medieval streets at dusk,
tangled in awe or poisoned by argument.

Or along pure mountain streams
where bamboo trembles as an afterthought.
Our places never disappear,

only the wind without destination
like us among fellow passengers
stranded in a world that won't let go.

Love Songs in Another Language

Her name has the sea in it.
And the word for sailor.
It could've been a cloud, a precious stone,
the chaotic skywriting of the flock.
In the end it's about the tone
to grasp any real meaning.
A third character sounds like
the month of June.
Not soft, not like those reliable
summer nights, the kids
called from the pool
and some old guys
grumbling about the evening news
tap their pipes,
commiserating at the curb.
Her name has the word *when*
in it, too. When love songs in a language
you don't entirely understand
are still love songs,
and not the dumbfounded stare
of her boyfriend asking when
and where she got that tattoo?
Legs crisscrossed, indelicately composed,
arms thrown wide. Steady as she goes.
Not the same when—it isn't a question—
looking out at the open sea
never asking for anything.

Shadow Nation

I have been working away quietly, steadily
in a provisional state, in secret,
with only a few necessary things: a fountain pen,
books and music, unfinished poems,
and letters to friends.
You say you'd like more tangible proof.
Some belief perhaps in improvised prayer.
In my shadow nation
I am nomadic, never an exile.
I'd never keep a bird.
I like walking to the post office.
I like the mailbox
and the stamps. I travel fast, my bags are light,
trying to catch the morning flight.
Someday I'll slow down.
I'll look after myself
wherever I go, here or there,
to keep this feeling of light
the moment my body leaves the ground.

Today

When winter mornings stay darker
longer and the avenues
are still empty. Where the traffic lights
dangle like emeralds and rubies
for someone who squints.
When the pockets of morning sky
arrive like sapphires
you couldn't possibly carry.
The day is coming
when your superstitions will spit
in your face and laugh.
Like today
when you'll stop asking:
How many more days?

Notes Prior To Departure

Here's a red envelope
full of money for good luck.
I'm sorry it's not enough.
Here's the key to the mailbox.
It's the one like a silly Swiss chalet,
though it only brings the bills
or boring news—no mysteries there.
Help yourself to the fridge.
There you might find mysteries.
Don't drink all my liquor.
I'd recommend a modest glass
of bourbon after lunch and a nap.
The couch is too small
but I pretend to be a baby.
Pray for the family.
If you need something to love
spray and water the plants.
Some say poems of departure
are no longer relevant,
not since the Chinese left
to roam far beyond the mountains.
Walking deep into a mist
they slept above the clouds.

Tomorrow

Tomorrow with its false eyelashes
wants to keep its great secret:
It's always a little lovesick.
In fact, it despises you.
It comes like a bolt of lightning
that could split us in two.
No need to apologize.
It loves to tease yesterday's déjà vu.
Between now
and the day after tomorrow
we'll get along fine.
There's always tomorrow
for somebody else.

Turning

So goes the revolution. To turn the wheel,
to *rotate, revolve*, turning
the turn, the turn of a hair—and it's the loss
of all composure. A hairpin turn, to turnabout, to look …
Now it's your turn
to turn down, to spin, swivel, swerve—
to take the curve that turns
the stomach, to veer and arc,
with the turn of a screw
the turnbuckle of the body is fixed.
Turning the tables.
You're never turning back.
Turn the key as all heads turn,
when nobody is looking,
the body turned loose no longer impounded.
Turn up the music.
Turn off the lights.
Turn on. Turn over. We take turns
twirling before turning-in for the night,
to return to sleep,
to turn out with the morning riders
who, in turn, turn their pages.
Turn around and we turn a certain age.
Turn around again and the sunlight is turning,
turning this dim room bright.

People Like To Tell Me Things

Something about a birdcage
without its bird,

or a thousand pairs of hands

on which you could count the friendships
that have fallen off the map.

Europe, somebody says,
has nothing else to teach us.

Or how flamingos stand perfectly still
like question marks.

Like things that fall from the sky.
What if it was rice instead of rain?

People like to tell me things.

Late Summer Lament

First I pass the man having a morning smoke,
his cart filled with ripe melons.
Then a woman with her pyramids
of summer peaches.
They are the sweetest this time of year.
Then a basket of figs
I'm guessing from Wulumuqi
the color of fresh bruises,
the color of summer wounds
I hope will heal with time.
The cicadas are singing themselves to death,
because that's what they do
at this time of year.
And if just one of them was caged
to your ear you'd go deaf,
you'd think you are losing your mind.
I could think of nothing else:
twenty million baby rattles going insane,
twenty million cries for love
heard above rivers of bad traffic,
above the never-ending destruction
when I spot a bucket of coal
in the morning sun
and how its blackness glitters.

Anima Mundi

When a friend says she expects
a poem by Monday morning

she means something about the deer.
How they nibble the grass

as skittish as the poem
my friend expects. They want the grass,

and to graze in the neighbor's garden.
The salt lick they ignore.

We try to make sense of what is timid,
of what cannot be tamed—

twigs snapping underfoot
before an abrupt leap into a lace of sunlight.

The Corners

after Gaston Bachelard

Sometimes I imagine the corners
of a day or sometimes a month,
another year like mastering origami.

I prefer walking in cities where the streets
are named after philosophers.
Even the crows in Tokyo and Paris

seem to agree: We still live in a world
of questions. When I woke up
I was somewhere over the Black Sea.

Night School

An alarm goes off
as you stumble out of the dark
mood you took to bed.
When you find a note
at the kitchen table
written in the hand of a child
who is not a child.
Soon enough one learns to crawl
through a miniature world.
Soon enough you learn about ladders,
mirrors, lamplight, rain
and rumors, the wind,
and the ghosts in the wind.
You'll learn to listen to a lone bird
whose song pierces
whatever's left of this darkness
breaking open
which reminds you,
you still believe in luck.

NOTES

Weldon Kees's poem, in its entirety, which appears as the epigraph to this collection is titled "Small Prayer" and was written sometime between 1947 and 1954.

"Extended Lullaby" is titled after a composition by John Cage. The poem also references Cage's avid and longtime interest in mushroom hunting and mycology.

The poem "Giacometti's Nose" was written after reading James Lord's book *A Giacometti Portrait*, and from passages in translation from Jean Genet's book on the artist.

Early drafts of many of these poems were written in Shanghai, China between 2006 and 2018. "Friday, Night Shanghai" was among the first.

"Samuel Beckett's Tree," "What Is Not," "A Matter of Faith," and "Siddhartha On Fire" also appear in the chapbook *Siddhartha On Fire* published by Swan Scythe Press (2023), edited by Robert Pesich.

ACKNOWLEDGMENTS

Grateful acknowledgment is made to the editors of the following publications in which these poems first appeared:

The Antioch Review: "The Studio," "God and Windshield," "Friday Night, Shanghai"

Arts & Letters: "Samuel Beckett's Tree"

Barrow Street: "Where the Sky Meets the Sea"(4x2 online) and Barrow Street (print): "Because There's No Patron Saint for Chocolate," "Siddhartha On Fire"

BOMB: "Turning," "Utopia Parkway," "To Marie," "An Orchid for Robert Mapplethorpe"

Chelsea: "Giacometti's Nose"

Forklift, Ohio: "People Like To Tell Me Things"

Inverted Syntax: "Postcards"

Little Star: "Anima Mundi," "Airport Blues"

The London Magazine: "Mid-Autumn Moon," "The Weight of Every Possible Move," "Andaman Morning"

The Louisville Review: "Yellow," "Extended Lullaby"

The Manhattanville Review: "My Warhol"

Prairie Schooner: "Like Air"

The Rialto: "Shadow Nation"

Salmagundi: "Late Portrait," "Fu Xing Park"

The Shanghai Literary Review: "Rexroth's Dream"

Southern Poetry Review: "Notes Prior To Departure"

Tiferet: "Nietzsche's Ghazal"

TriQuarterly: "Love Songs in Another Language," "Late Summer Lament," "Today," "A Matter of Faith"

Tupelo Quarterly: "Skin Deep," "Remembering Steinberg," "Night School" (Winner of the Tupelo Press 2019 Broadside contest)

Waxing & Waning: "The Corners," "Until the Sun Comes Up"

Thanks also to *Poetry Daily* for posting "Turning" which originally appeared in *BOMB* and to the Academy of American Poets for posting "What Is Not" on *Poem-a-Day*.

There are a number of people who helped to make this book possible. My endless gratitude to both Marianne Boruch and Forrest Gander. Many thanks to Lise Goett and Maggie Smith for their insights and invaluable guidance. Special thanks to Robert and Peg Boyers, Reginald Gibbons, Brett Hall Jones at the Community of Writers, Judith Hall, Robert Hass and Brenda Hillman. Also a special thanks to Lorenz Helbling at ShangART Gallery and artist Yang Fudong for the use of his film still from *Seven Intellectuals in a Bamboo Forest* for the cover art. My sincere gratitude to Katie Farris and Ilya Kaminsky, and to Frank Majore, Magdalena Montagne, Juli Min, and to Betsy Sussler. My wholehearted thanks to the Warren Wilson MFA Program for Writers and to my fellow graduates, teachers and mentors. Lastly, my profound and heartfelt thanks to Leah Huete de Maines for her faith in this book and to Kevin Maines and the entire team at Finishing Line Press.

This book is dedicated to the memory of Mark Strand.

Arthur Solway's poetry and essays have appeared in *The Antioch Review, Barrow Street, BOMB, The London Magazine, Salmagundi, Southern Poetry Review, TriQuarterly*, and elsewhere. His work has also been featured by the Academy of American Poets Poem-a-Day. His critical reviews and cultural essays can be found in *Artforum, Frieze,* and *ArtAsiaPacific* magazines. Living and working in Shanghai for well over a decade, he was the founding director of the first contemporary art gallery from New York to establish itself in mainland China. A graduate of the Warren Wilson MFA Program for Writers, he is a poetry editor for *The Shanghai Literary Review* and presently lives in Santa Cruz, California.

www.ingramcontent.com/pod-product-compliance
Lightning Source LLC
Chambersburg PA
CBHW020811160426
43192CB00006B/520